Anthology No. 1: Melody

Follow this skeleton score as you listen to an old French carol.

Quit - tez, pas - teurs, Vos bre - bis, vos hou -
- let - tes, Vo - tre ha - meau, Et le soin du trou -
- peau; Chan - gez vos pleurs En u - ne joie par -
- fai - te; Al - lez tous a - do - rer Un Dieu, un
Dieu, un Dieu qui vient vous con - so - ler.

Here are the words and a translation:

Quittez, pasteurs	**Shepherds, leave**
Vos brebis, vos houlettes	**Your lambs, your crooks,**
Votre hameau	**Your hamlet,**
Et le soin du troupeau;	**And the care of the flock;**
Changez vos pleurs	**Change your tears**
En une joie parfaite;	**Into perfect joy;**
Allez tous adorer	**Go, all of you, and worship**
Un Dieu qui vient vous consoler	**A God who comes to console you.**

1 Insert an appropriate time signature at the beginning.
2 Complete the melody in bars 10-12.
3 In which bars is a phrase of the melody repeated?
4 In which bars can you hear a complete descending scale?
5 What sort of scale is it?
6 What type of voice is singing the melody?

Anthology No. 2: Melody

Here are the words and a translation of a comic Dutch song.

Komt hier al'bij, aanhoort dees Klucht	**Come all near and hear this farce**
Het is van Pierlala,	**It's all about Pierlala,**
Een drollig ventjen vol genucht,	**A witty chap well enough,**
De vreugd van zijn papa.	**The joy of his Dad.**
Wat in zijn Leven is geschied,	**Something that happened in his life**
Dat zult gij hooren in dit lied:	**You shall hear in this song:**
'tIs al van Pierlala.	**It's all about Pierlala.**

Listen to this song with the printed music then answer the following questions.

1 How many beats are there in each bar?
2 What is the length of each beat?
3 What sort of scale is this melody based on?
4 There are four phrases in this song. Write down four letters to show which phrases are repeated (e.g. **ABBA** would show that the first phrase is repeated at the end, and that the second phrase is repeated immediately).
5 In which of these phrases is there a sequence?

Anthology No. 3: Melody

LISTENING WITHOUT PRINTED MUSIC

1 Which one of these terms best describes the type of scale upon which this melody is built: a), b), c), or d)?
   a) pentatonic
   b) major
   c) minor
   d) modal
2 What type of voice is singing the melody?
3 There are some big leaps in this melody. Name the large rising interval heard at the start. Name one other large rising interval in the middle of the song.
4 Name this type of song.

LISTENING WITH PRINTED MUSIC

1 On which word does the climax of this song occur?
2 Describe two ways in which the music emphasizes this climax.
3 Which phrase is repeated with only slight modifications?

Anthology No. 4: Melody

LISTENING WITHOUT PRINTED MUSIC

1 How many beats are there in each bar?
2 Which one of these terms best describes the type of scale upon which this tune is built: a), b), c), or d)?
   a) minor
   b) pentatonic
   c) major
   d) modal
3 What type of voice is singing the tune?
4 How does the singer produce the interruptions in the sound of the very last note of the song?
5 From which of these peoples do you think this tune came: a), b), c), or d)?
   a) Australian Aborigines
   b) North American Indians
   c) South African Bushmen
   d) Alaskan Eskimos

LISTENING WITH PRINTED MUSIC

1 How would you describe the rhythm in bars 2, 4, 6, 8 and 10?
2 Apart from the last bar, this song falls into two-bar phrases. Write down a series of five letters to show the order in which these two-bar phrases are repeated.

Anthology No. 5: Harmony and Rhythm

1 This music begins with an elaborate solo for the crumhorn. What name would you give to the accompaniment to this solo?
2 The music ends with a section of full harmony. Which of these terms best describes this harmony: a), b), c), or d)?
    a) discordant
    b) concordant
    c) chromatic
    d) atonal
3 Is this music in the major, the minor, or no key at all?

1 How does the harmony of bars 1-16 differ from that of bars 17-32?
2 Name the cadences in a) bars 19-20 and
                               b) bars 23-24.
3 Describe one important difference between the rhythm of the crumhorn solo at the beginning of this music and the rhythm of the following sections which are printed in your book.
4 In the performance of bars 17-32 does the music
    a) maintain a steady tempo
    b) speed up, or
    c) slow down?

Anthology No. 6: Melody and Texture

1 This music is for four-part choir. What sort of voice, normally present in a mixed choir like this, is not used in this music?
2 Listen to the highest voice singing the word *Benedictus* (Blessed is He) at the beginning. Which TWO of the following terms best describe Palestrina's melody for this word?
    a) chromatic (using notes not belonging to the scale)
    b) melismatic (having several notes sung to one syllable)
    c) syncopated (having accents off the beat or on a weak beat)
    d) disjunct (moving by leaps)
    e) conjunct (moving by steps)
    f) triadic (moving up and down thirds and fourths to outline chords)
3 After the word *Benedictus* has been heard several times, one of the voices begins singing *qui venit* (who comes) to this fragment of melody:

What do the other voices do when they sing the same words?
4 In the next section the top voice sings *in nomine Domini* (in the name of the Lord), starting very high up. Which one of these diagrams represents the correct shape of the melody at this point: a), b), c), or d)?

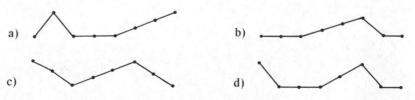

5 At the very end there is a plagal cadence. The texture here could be described as homophonic or chordal: how would you describe the texture of all the music before this cadence?

Anthology No. 7: Melody and Texture

Here is the text, with a translation:

O quam gloriosum est regnum	**O how glorious is the kingdom**
In quo cum Christo gaudent	**In which there rejoice with Christ**
Omnes Sancti!	**All the Saints!**
Amicti stolis albis	**Clothed in white robes**
Sequuntur Agnum	**They follow the Lamb**
Quocunque ierit.	**Wherever he goes.**

1 In the first phrase (bars 1-9) there are two contrasting textures. Describe the texture in
   a) bars 1-4,
   b) bars 5-9.
2 How does Victoria's setting of the first two syllables of *gloriosum* (bars 4-6) differ from his setting of the third syllable?
3 Listen to bars 10-13, then answer the following questions.
   a) Which part sings the same four notes as those sung by the bass in bars 10^2-11^1?
   b) Which part begins to sing the same melody as that sung by the tenor in bars 9^4-11^1?
   c) What is the difference between the melody you found in answer to question b) and the tenor melody in bars 9^4-11^1?
   d) Which one of the following terms best describes bars 10-13?
      i) canon
      ii) fugue
      iii) imitation
      iv) sequence
4 What in the music suggests
   a) rejoicing at the word *gaudent* (bars 18^4-22)?
   b) the idea of people following each other at the words *sequuntur Agnum* (bars 35^4-46)?

Anthology No. 8: Instruments and Voices

LISTENING
WITHOUT
PRINTED
MUSIC

1 This music begins with a passage for instruments alone. Give the names of the instruments: a), b), c) and d).

    a) a wind instrument

    b) a bowed treble string instrument

    c) a bowed bass string instrument

    d) a plucked string instrument

2 Which one of these names most accurately describes the instrumental group: a), b), c), or d)?

    a) orchestra

    b) consort

    c) quartet

    d) band

3 Which one of these names most accurately describes the vocal group: a), b), c), or d)?

    a) male-voice choir

    b) mixed choir

    c) opera chorus

    d) solo vocal ensemble

4 This music comes from the Elizabethan period.

    a) What type of music is it?

    b) Suggest a composer who might have written it.

    c) Give one reason why it is clearly from this period.

LISTENING
WITH
PRINTED
MUSIC

1 The letters below represent the five sections of this music. Complete the table, following the examples which have been given:

    A instruments alone (bars 1-10)

    B voices and instruments together (bars 11-19)

    B^1

    A^1

    A

2 In which bars do the voices imitate each other?

Anthology No. 9: Instruments, Voices and Texture

LISTENING
WITHOUT
PRINTED
MUSIC

1 All of these following words or phrases accurately describe parts of the music.
   a) chorus
   b) unaccompanied
   c) homophonic (chordal)
   d) chant
   e) orchestra alone
   f) solo
   g) with orchestra

The three clear sections into which this music is divided are represented below as i), ii) and iii). Choosing from the list above, write appropriate words and/or phrases against these sections to describe them.

Section i)...

Section ii) ....

Section iii) ....

2 Name three instruments playing in this music

LISTENING
WITH
PRINTED
MUSIC

Here is the text, with a translation:

Deus in adjutorium meum intende: **O God, come to my assistance:**
Domine ad adjuvandum me festina.   **O Lord, make haste to help me.**

1 Which one of these words best describes the way in which the first line of the text is sung: a), b), c), or d)?
   a) ornamented
   b) intoned
   c) declaimed
   d) monotoned

2 Choose one word from the list above to describe the way in which every voice in the chorus sings.

3 In which bars and in which instruments can you hear a canon?

Anthology No. 10: Melody, Harmony and Form

1 Here is the melody you will hear in the first phrase, together with the beginning of the bass part (which is played by a cello):

Complete the bass part and name the chords: they are all in root position except for the chord labelled I*b* (this is a first inversion of the tonic chord; that is, with the third of the chord as the bass note instead of the root).

2 Name the cadence in the fourth bar.

3 To which of these keys does the music modulate in the second four-bar phrase: a), b), or c)?

    a) the subdominant

    b) the dominant

    c) the relative minor

1 You can see that there are two sections in this piece, and both are marked to be repeated. In what ways do the violin melodies differ from your printed score when they are repeated?

2 In what key does the music begin and end?

3 To what key does the music modulate in bar 12?

4 Which one of these words most accurately describes the form of this music: a), b), c), or d)?

    a) binary

    b) ternary

    c) sonata form

    d) rondo

Anthology No. 11: Rhythm, Instruments and Melody

LISTENING
WITHOUT
PRINTED
MUSIC

1 Suggest an appropriate time signature for this music.
2 Which two of the following rhythms can you hear in the instrumental introduction?

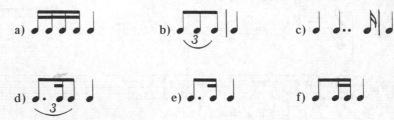

3 Name the two instruments which play together at the beginning before the
   violins come in.
4 Which of these is the correct term for the part from which both of these
   instruments read: a), b), c), or d)?
   a) ripieno
   b) tutti
   c) concertino
   d) basso continuo
5 Describe the bass part in the whole extract.
6 What name is given to this sort of bass part?

LISTENING
WITH
PRINTED
MUSIC

1 In which bars do the recorders and violins play antiphonally?
2 In which bars do the voices imitate each other?
3 In what way does the repeat of bars 26-42 differ from the music you heard
   when it was first performed?

4 If ♩. = ♩ ♪ , what combination of tied notes is equivalent to the double-
   dotted crotchet in bar 7? Answer the question by completing this formula:

   ♩.. =

Anthology No. 12: Texture, Counterpoint and Form

LISTENING WITHOUT PRINTED MUSIC

1 The texture of this movement alternates between the full sound of a string orchestra and the thinner sound of a group of a soloists. What are the proper names for these groups?

2 In the first section for full string orchestra you will hear a theme in the bass instruments accompanied by an organ only. How many more times is this complete theme played in this section? How do these repetitions differ from the theme as first played by the bass instruments?

LISTENING WITH PRINTED MUSIC

1 In which bars and on which instruments is a counter-subject played against the theme?

2 Name the pattern made by the descending scales in bars 64-65.

3 In which bars does Vivaldi invert these scales?

4 What name would you give to the sustained bass note in bars 89-100?

5 How does the texture of the last two bars differ from the rest of the movement?

6 Which of the following words best describes the form of this music: a), b), c), or d)?

    a) variations

    b) fugue

    c) ternary

    d) passacaglia

7 From which of the following types of work might this movement have been taken: a), b), c), or d)?

    a) concerto grosso

    b) suite

    c) trio sonata

    d) solo concerto

Anthology No. 13: Melody, Harmony and Form

Here is the text, with a translation:

Lascia ch'io pianga la cruda sorte,   **Let me lament my cruel fate**
E che sospiri la liberta!   **And sigh for freedom!**
Il duolo infranga questi ritorti,   **May grief shatter these bonds,**
De' miei martiri sol per pieta.   **Release me from my torments, if only**
                                          for pity's sake.

LISTENING
WITHOUT
PRINTED
MUSIC

1 What type of voice sings this melody?
2 Here is the melody of the first eight bars. Write V and I under the melody at the two places where you hear perfect cadences:

3 Here is part of the melody of the third and fourth lines of the text. Complete the melody in the blank bars.

4 In what key does this melody begin?
5 Apart from the key, how does Handel's setting of the third and fourth lines of the text differ from his setting of the first and second lines?

LISTENING
WITH
PRINTED
MUSIC

1 If the eight-bar phrase given under question 2 above can be represented by the letter **A**, write down a series of four letters to represent the form of the first thirty bars.
2 Which of these words best describes the form of the whole movement as you have heard it on the recording: a), b), c), or d)?
   a) passacaglia
   b) ternary
   c) fugue
   d) variations

[12]

Anthology No. 14: Bass and Harmony

LISTENING WITHOUT PRINTED MUSIC

1 After hearing the whole extract, listen several times to just the first five bars. The bass part in these bars begins and ends like this:

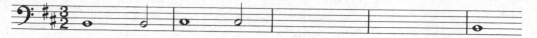

Complete this bass melody as you listen to it.

2 Listen to the whole extract again. You will notice that the bass part of the first four bars is repeated twice, the first time with a choir, the second time with violins. After this the bass is altered. How does the repeated bass melody in the second half of the extract differ from the bass melody of the first four bars?

LISTENING WITH PRINTED MUSIC

1 Name the chords used above the last four bass notes of the extract (bars 24-25).

2 What sort of cadence do the last two chords make?

3 What do the figures under the bass part mean?

4 What harmony instrument can you hear which is not represented in the score? It can clearly be heard on the first chord.

5 What name would you give to a composition that, like this one, has a repeating bass melody above which there are various other melodies and harmonies?

6 From what sort of work might this chorus have been taken? The translation of the text might help you:

Meine Tage in den Leiden	**My days spent in suffering**
Endet Gott dennoch zu Freuden.	**God yet ends in joy.**

Anthology No. 15: Melody

LISTENING
WITHOUT
PRINTED
MUSIC

1 Which one of these words best describes the melodies: a), b), c), or d?
   a) diatonic
   b) atonal
   c) chromatic
   d) pentatonic
2 Which one of these words could also be used to describe the melodies: a), b), c), d)?
   a) smooth
   b) conjunct
   c) disjunct
   d) calm
3 Name the solo melody instrument.
4 Name the type of voice.
5 What are the other two instruments, which accompany the two soloists?
6 Which one of these is the correct term for this accompaniment: a), b), c) or d)?
   a) Basso continuo
   b) orchestra
   c) chamber ensemble
   d) consort
7 How does the bass melody differ from the soloists' melodies?

LISTENING
WITH
PRINTED
MUSIC

1 What does the time signature indicate?
2 Name the unusual interval, E flat–B natural, in the first beat.
3 Where, in the first four bars, is there a sequence?
4 This music is often dissonant. Name the type of dissonance formed by the voice against the accompaniment in the last bar before the D.C.
5 How does Bach express the meaning of the text (see below) in his music?

Seufzer, Tränen, Kummer, Not,
Ängstlich's Sehnen, Furcht und Tod
Nagen mein beklemmtes Herz,
Ich empfinde Jammer, Schmerz.

Sighs, tears, sorrow, need,
Anxious yearning, fear and death
Gnaw at my tormented heart,
Misery and pain I know.

Anthology Nos. 16a and 16b: Tonality, Melody and Form

Here is a translation of the text of the vocal composition which you will hear first (No. 16a):

Erschienen ist der herrliche Tag,
D'ran sich Niemand g'nug freuen mag:
Christ, unser Herr, heut triumphirt,
All' sein' Feind'er gefangen fürht.

The day of splendour has arrived,
Call no one's joy at this too great;
Christ, our Lord, triumphant today
Leads all his enemies captive.

LISTENING WITHOUT PRINTED MUSIC

Listen to both the vocal composition and the organ piece before answering the following questions.

1 Which of these words best describes the tonality of the first piece: a), b), c), or d)?
  a) major
  b) pentatonic
  c) minor
  d) bitonal

2 What sort of group performs the first piece?

3 Where, in both pieces, can you hear a *tierce de Picardie*?

4 What is the connection between the two pieces?

5 Which one of these terms most accurately describes the first piece: a), b), c), or d)?
  a) hymn
  b) chorus
  c) chorale
  d) aria

6 Which one of these terms most accurately describes the second piece: a), b), c), or d)?
  a) fugue
  b) chorale prelude
  c) fantasia
  d) toccata

7 Here are the first two phrases of the uppermost part of the second piece. Ten notes have been missed out: write these notes in as you listen to the tune.

8 Which one of these words best describes the tonality of this melody: a), b), c), or d)?
  a) major
  b) modal
  c) polytonal
  d) minor

9 What connection is there between this tune and the tune played on the organ pedals (i.e. the bass part)?

Anthology No. 17: Ornamentation and Form

1 Listen to the first sixteen bars and give the bar numbers in which you hear the following ornaments.
   a) a turn
   b) a mordent
   c) a short trill

2 Listen to the first sixteen bars again: they divide into two eight-bar phrases. Compare these two phrases.

3 What sort of cadence can you hear at the end of this first sixteen-bar section?

4 Listen to the first twenty-four bars. What cadence can you hear at the end of this section?

5 Now listen to the first forty bars. What do you notice about bars 25-40?

6 Listen to bars 41-48. The music modulates in these bars. To which key does it modulate? What sort of cadence can you hear in bars 47-48?

7 Now listen to the whole piece and write down a series of letters to represent the form of the whole movement. You will need a series to represent the five sections which are divided from each other by the double bars.

8 Which one of these words most accurately describes the form which you have represented by a series of letters: a), b), c), or d)?
   a) binary
   b) rondo
   c) ternary
   d) variations

Anthology No. 18: Rhythm, Melody and Form

LISTENING
WITHOUT
PRINTED
MUSIC

1 Suggest a suitable time signature for this music.
2 Which of these rhythms corresponds with the rhythm of the melody in the first two beats of the music: a), b), c), or d)?

    a)   b)   c)   d)

3 Which instruments play this rhythm?
4 Which solo instrument plays a completely different rhythm later on in the movement?
5 Which one of the following series of letters corresponds with the overall form of the whole piece: i), ii), iii), or iv)?
    i) **ABA**
    ii) **AAB**
    iii) **ABB**
    iv) **ABC**

LISTENING
WITH
PRINTED
MUSIC

1 What do you notice about the rhythm of the first two beats of bars 1, 2, 3, 5, 9 and 10?
2 What key is this piece in?
3 To what key does it modulate at bar 4?
4 In which bar is the melody of the first two beats of bar 1 repeated? In which bar is it transposed?
5 Which one of the following series of letters corresponds with the form of the first twelve bars (including the repeats): i), ii), iii), iv)?
    i) **ABA**
    ii) **ABCA**
    iii) **AABA^{1}BA^1**
    iv) **ABA^{1}CA^{1}BA**
6 Compare the cello (basso continuo) melody of bars 13-24 with the flute melody of bars 1-12. What do you notice?
7 Which of these words best describes the flute solo: a), b), c), or d)?
    a) descant
    b) fauxbourdon
    c) stretto
    d) counter-melody
8 *Double* is a French word. What do you think it means?

Anthology No. 19: Rhythm and Texture

LISTENING
WITHOUT
PRINTED
MUSIC

1 This music divides into three sections: two solo sections and a chorus. What type of voice sings the solo sections?

2 Both of the solo sections are recitatives: that is, music in which a story is told by a soloist almost as fast as in normal speech. In what ways do these recitatives differ from each other in
- a) rhythm?
- b) instrumentation?

3 Which instruments are added in the chorus?

LISTENING
WITH
PRINTED
MUSIC

1 What instruments play from the *basso continuo* part in the first (*secco*) recitative?

2 What instruments that are normally used in a continuo are omitted in the second (*accompagnato*) recitative?

3 Which voice part does Handel omit from the chorus in the first four bars?

4 Read the text then give a reason for the omissions in both the second recitative and the chorus.

5 In which bars of the chorus can you hear each of the following textures:
- a) repeated string chords?
- b) fugato?
- c) four-voice homophony?
- d) three-part string texture without continuo or chorus?

Anthology No. 20: Orchestration and Form

1 Listen to the music all the way through. There is a long section in F minor, a shorter middle section, then a repeat of the first section. In what key is the short middle section? In what form is the whole movement? In what form is the short middle section?

2 The F minor section alternates between loud and soft. What wind instruments double the violins' tune in the loud passages?

3 Listen again to the F minor section. To which one of these keys does it first modulate: i), ii), or iii)?
   i) C minor
   ii) A flat major
   iii) E flat major

4 Listen to the middle section as you follow the uppermost oboe part, printed below (keep counting in the blank bars!). Then answer the questions below.

   a) Complete the melody in bars 63-68.
   b) What instrument plays the snippet of melody given on the second stave in bars 56-57?
   c) In which bars can you hear a tonic pedal?

5 From what type of work might this movement have been taken?

Anthology No. 21: Variations

1 Complete the melody of the first eight bars on the stave below.

2 What sort of cadence is used at *x*, and what different cadence is used at *y*?

3 In what key does this melody begin, and to what key has it modulated at *y*?

4 To which one of these keys does the music modulate in the four-bar phrase immediately following bar 8: i), ii), or iii)?
    i) F major
    ii) E flat major
    iii) C minor

1 In what form is Haydn's theme (bars 1-20)?

2 Compare the first four bars of the theme (bars 1-4) with the first four bars of Variation 1 (bars 21-24).
    a) Put a cross (in soft pencil) above each note in the variation which corresponds with a note in the theme. Describe how Haydn has varied the theme in bars 21-24.
    b) Compare the cello parts in both sets of bars. What do you notice?

3 Compare the cello part in bars 1-4 with the cello part in the first four bars of Variation 2. What do you notice?

4 In what way are Variations 1, 2, and 3 almost exactly the same as the theme?

Anthology No. 22: Form and Orchestration

Listen to the beginning of this extract as you follow the skeleton score below, then answer the questions.

1 What keyboard instrument plays the melody in bars 74-76?
2 What wind instrument doubles this keyboard melody?
3 What instrument plays the upper part given in bar 77?
4 What instrument plays the tune given in the first half of bar 78, and which one plays the scale in the second half?
5 Which previous bar is repeated in the blank bar 79?
6 Which instrument plays a tonic pedal in semiquavers in bars 78-79?
7 Which family of instruments accompanies the keyboard in bars 80-81?
8 Which previous bars are repeated in bars 82-85?
9 Which instrument plays the broken chords in bars 85-88?
10 From what part of the movement is this extract taken?
11 From what sort of work might this be the second movement?

Anthology No. 23: Words and Music

LISTENING
WITHOUT
PRINTED
MUSIC

During the orchestral prelude to this song Papageno (the singer) comes down a footpath with a huge birdcage on his back. He is covered with feathers and plays an instrument as he enters.
Then he sings the following:

1 *Der Vogelfänger bin ich ja,*
Stets lustig, heisa hopsasa!
Ich Vogelfänger bin bekannt
Bei Alt und Jung im ganzen Land.

Weiss mit dem Locken umzugehn,
Und mich auf's Pfeifen zu verstehn!
D'rum kann ich froh und lustig sein,
Denn alle Vögel sind ja mein.

2 *Der Vogelfänger bin ich ja,*
Stets lustig, heisa hopsasa!
Ich Vogelfänger bin bekannt
Bei Alt und Jung im ganzen Land.

Ein Netz für Mädchen möchte ich,
Ich fing' sie dutzendweis' für mich!
Dann sperrte ich sie bei mir ein,
Und alle Mädchen wären mein.

3 *Wenn alle Mädchen wären mein,*
So tauschte ich brav Zucker ein:
Die, welche mir am liebsten wär',
Der gäb' ich gleich den Zucker her.
Und küsste sie mich zärtlich dann,
Wär' sie mein Weib und ich ihr Mann.
Sie schlief' an meiner Seite ein,
Ich wiegte wie ein Kind sie ein.

1 Oh yes, I am the bird-catcher,
Ever jolly, hey up we go!
Now I, bird-catcher, am well known
By young and old throughout the land.
I know how to handle the lure,
I'm a dab hand at whistling too!
So I can be glad and jolly,
'Cos all the birds of course are mine.

2 Oh yes, I am the bird-catcher,
Ever jolly, hey up we go!
Now I, bird-catcher, am well known
By young and old throughout the land.
I'd like a net for catching girls,
Then I'd catch them by the dozen!
I'd lock them up with me at home,
And then ev'ry girl would be mine.

3 If then ev'ry girl would be mine,
Kind me would swap a sugar-lump:
The one who was sweetest to me
I'd hand my little sweetie to.
Then if she kissed me tenderly,
She'd be my wife and I her man.
She'd fall asleep beside me here
I'd rock her to sleep like a child.

1 What instrument does Papageno play? It is the only instrument played without accompaniment in this music.
2 What type of voice does Papageno have?
3 What do you notice about the music for verses 2 and 3?
4 Which of the following most accurately describes the music: a), b), c), or d)?
   a) air
   b) *lied*
   c) strophic song
   d) recitative
5 From what larger work might this music have been taken?

Anthology No. 24: Sonata Form

1 Name each of the following main sections of the movement:
   a) bars 1-33
   b) bars 33-63
   c) bars 64-103
   d) bars 103-110
2 Complete the following analysis by filling in the blanks.

Bars	Sections	Keys
1-15	first subject	G minor modulating to chord V of B flat major at bar 15
16-33		
33-38	development (1)	modulates from B flat major to E flat major
38-46	development (2)	
46-50	development (3)	sequential modulation to C minor
50-54	development (4)	
54-63	development (5)	dominant preparation
64-79		G minor with a transitory modulation to B flat major (bars 75-76)
80-103		
103-110		

Anthology No. 25: Orchestral Textures

Listen to the music as you follow the main melodic line printed below, then answer the questions.

1 How do bars 1-2 differ in instrumentation from bars 3-4?
2 Which one of these terms best describes the texture of bars 3-4: a), b), c), or d)?
    a) homophonic
    b) unison
    c) contrapuntal
    d) accompanied
3 How does the texture of bars 3-4 differ from the texture of bars 1-2?
4 Which family of instruments is playing in bar 9?
5 What sort of instruments are playing the solo parts in bars 10-25? How many of these instruments are playing in bar 10, and how many in bar 24?
6 Which one of these words accurately describes the way the violins and violas are played in bar 25: a), b), c), or d)?
    a) tremolo
    b) sul tasto
    c) muted
    d) pizzicato
7 Which of the above words describes how the double basses are played in bar 26?
8 Which section of the orchestra plays the tune from bar 27?

Anthology No. 26: Words and Music

Here is the text and a translation of a song by Schubert:

1 *Das Meer erglänzte weit hinaus*

   Im letzten Abendscheine.
   Wir sassen am einsamen Fischerhaus,

   Wir sassen stumm und alleine.

2 *Der Nebel stieg, das Wasser schwoll,*
   Die Möwe flog hin und wieder.
   Aus deinen Augen liebevoll
   Fielen die Tränen nieder.

3 *Ich sah sie fallen auf deine Hand*
   Und bin aufs Knie gesunken.
   Ich hab von deiner weissen Hand
   Die Tränen fortgetrunken.

4 *Seit jener Stunde verzehrt sich mein Leib,*
   Die Seele stirbt vor Sehnen.
   Mich hat das unglücksel'ge Weib
   Vergiftet mit ihren Tränen.

1 **The sea was gleaming away into the distance**
In the last rays of evening.
We sat by the lonely fisherman's cottage,
We sat silent and alone.

2 **The mist rose up, the water swelled,**
The gull flew by now and again.
Lovingly from your eyes
Did tears flow down.

3 **I saw them falling on your** hand
And fell upon my knee.
From your white hand did I
Drink away those tears.

4 **From that hour my body languishes,**

My soul dies with longing.
The hapless girl has
Poisoned me with her tears.

1 Which one of these words describes the very first chord: a), b), c), or d)?
   a) minor
   b) chromatic
   c) major
   d) diatonic
2 Which one of the four words above best describes the harmony Schubert uses for the first verse?
3 In what ways do the harmonies and textures change to reflect the change of mood in the second verse?
4 How does Schubert draw attention to these underlined syllables in the second verse: *'Aus deinen Augen liebevoll fielen die Tränen nieder'*?
5 What do you notice about Schubert's setting of the third and fourth verses?

Anthology No. 27: Instruments, Rhythm and Tonality

1 What plucked string instruments can you hear near the beginning?

2 When you first hear these plucked instruments do they play: a), b), or c)?
    a) block chords
    b) scales
    c) a melody?

3 When these plucked instruments are not playing, the violins slide down the interval of a third (the effect is clearer the second time). Which one of the following is the correct term for this effect: a), b), c), or d)?
    a) glissando or *portamento*
    b) harmonics
    c) *sul ponticello*
    d) *arco*

4 In this same middle section the tempo changes. Which one of these words describes the change: a), b), c), or d)?
    a) *accelerando*
    b) *largo*
    c) *rallentando*
    d) *presto*

5 Suggest a suitable time signature for the music.

6 This music is supposed to describe an animated scene in a ballroom. Which of these terms is correct for this sort of descriptive music: a), b), c), or d)?
    a) symphonic music
    b) Impressionist music
    c) programme music
    d) Expressionist music

7 What sort of dance is the composer trying to portray?

8 Which one of these words best describes the way the woodwind play their ascending scale at the end of the extract: a), b), c), or d)?
    a) staccato
    b) legato
    c) *pesante*
    d) *mesto*

9 This extract begins in A major. What key does it finish in?

Anthology No. 28: Rhythm, Harmony and Melody

LISTENING
WITHOUT
PRINTED
MUSIC

1 Suggest a suitable tempo mark.
2 Which of these words best describes the way in which the pianist plays this music: a), b), c) or d)?
  a) *ritenuto*
  b) *rubato*
  c) *rigoroso*
  d) *risoluto*
3 Which one of these dances is this: a), b), c), or d)?
  a) minuet
  b) sarabande
  c) polonaise
  d) mazurka
4 Describe the four-bar introduction before the tune begins.
5 Here are the first four bars of the melody:

Describe what happens in the next four bars.
6 Describe the relationship between the next eight bars of melody and the first eight bars of the melody.
7 What happens in the remainder of the recorded performance?
8 With the exception of one chord (VI) this music is harmonized with only two chords. What are they?
9 The recording is a complete performance of this piece. What is unusual about the end of it?
10 Who do you think wrote it: Schubert, Chopin or Schumann?

Anthology No. 29: Melody and Form

LISTENING
WITH
PRINTED
MUSIC

On paper this music looks like a clarinet solo with a broken-chord accompaniment for the piano. If you listen very carefully, however, you will hear that it is more like a duet between the clarinet and the right-hand part of the piano. The melody line in the piano is indicated by the notes with stems pointing upwards. The questions are about both of these melody lines.

1 Explain the key signature of three flats in the clarinet part.
2 What is the interval between the first two notes of the piano melody?
3 What is the relationship between these two notes (in question 2) and the first two notes the clarinet plays?
4 Can you find any more phrases in the clarinet and piano parts which begin with the same interval?
5 Which of these terms best describes the relationship between the clarinet's phrase in bars 10^4-12^1 and the next phrase it plays (bars 12^2-13^1): a), b), c), or d)?
  a) augmentation
  b) inversion
  c) diminution
  d) retrograde
6 A middle section begins at bar 21 with some of the same melodic ideas, but from bar 27 real melodies disappear. What replaces them?
7 Follow just the clarinet part. In which bar does a repeat of the first nineteen bars begin?
8 Name, or describe, the form of this piece.

[27]

Anthology No. 30: Virtuosity

1 The seven paragraphs below describe seven different types of very difficult piano writing, but they are out of order. Listen to the music several times, then rearrange **A** to **G** into the order in which you hear these features occurring in the piece.

    A Eight-note chromatic chords in both hands.

    B A rising chromatic sequence in semiquavers with an ascending chromatic scale in quavers beneath it.

    C A decorated plagal cadence covering nearly the whole range of the keyboard.

    D A low, bare, double octave followed by a descending arpeggio of the dominant seventh in free rhythm.

    E Rising and falling diatonic arpeggios accompanied by block chords.

    F A diatonic semiquaver pattern repeated several times at a very high pitch with descending chords beneath it.

    G A series of trills moving downwards in the bass.

2 Which one of these words would you choose as a title for this piece: a), b), c), or d)?

    a) study

    b) sonata

    c) scherzo

    d) serenade

3 What is virtuosity?

Anthology No. 31: Words and Music

Here is the text and a translation of a duet:

Manrico *Sconto col sangue mio* — I am paying with my life- blood
L'amor che posi in te — For the love which I placed in you!
Non ti scordar di me? — You will not forget me?

Leonora, addio! — Farewell, Leonora!
Leonora *Di te scordarmi!* — Forget you!
Sento mancarmi. — I feel faint.
Chorus *Miserere!* — Have mercy!

1 What type of voice does Manrico have?
2 What instrument accompanies Manrico's solo at the beginning of this extract?
3 When Manrico first sings his top note, very near the beginning of the extract, he scoops up to it to make it sound more passionate. Which one of these words correctly describes this vocal technique: a), b), c), or d)?
   a) *parlando*
   b) *portamento*
   c) *legato*
   d) *sotto voce*
4 Just before Leonora first sings, Manrico alters the tempo of the music. Describe this alteration.
5 What type of voice does Leonora have?
6 At what point does the full orchestra first enter?
7 If you listen very carefully you will just be able to hear the chorus. What sort of chorus is it?
8 This music begins in A flat major. In which key does it end?
9 From what sort of work do you think this music is taken?
10 Which one of the following is the most likely composer?
   a) Weber
   b) Verdi
   c) Wagner
   d) Puccini

Anthology No. 32: Instrumentation and Harmony

The music below shows the uppermost notes of the whole extract. Follow it as you listen and answer the questions as the music is repeated for you.

1 Which instrument or group of instruments play the notes printed above in:
   a) bar 1?
   b) bars 2-3?
2 Which family of instruments plays in:
   a) bar 13?
   b) bar 14?
   c) bar 15?
3 Which of these terms best describes the music in bars 13-15: a), b), c), or d)?
   a) imitation
   b) dialogue
   c) antiphony
   d) fugato
4 Which brass instrument can be heard clearly in bar 16?
5 Which one of these words best describes the chord in bar 2: a), b), c), or d)?
   a) common
   b) chromatic
   c) primary
   d) diatonic
6 In which bar is the chord, first heard in bar 2, repeated in sequence?

Anthology No. 33: Variations

LISTENING
WITHOUT
PRINTED
MUSIC

This extract is taken from a set of variations. The first three variations are all joined together, but the last variation is separated by a pause during which only the lower string instruments are heard holding a chord very quietly. Listen very carefully to the differences between the variations before the pause and the variation after it, then answer the following questions.

1 How does the last variation differ from the others in volume?
2 How does the last variation differ from the others in tempo?
3 How does the last variation differ from the others in key?
4 How does the last variation differ from the others in instrumentation?

LISTENING
WITH
PRINTED
MUSIC

1 At bar 112 you will hear an oboe playing a descending scale. Name the two other wind instruments which repeat this scale later in the extract.
2 Play the following bass melody by J.S. Bach, or ask your teacher to play it for you (you may have heard it already in an earlier class):

Listen to the music after the double bar, comparing it with the melody above. Now answer the following.
   a) Name one instrument which plays a version of the bass melody printed above.
   b) In what ways does the version of the melody in your score differ from the bass melody printed above?
3 Listen again to the music after the double bar. Which instruments play an extended version of the descending scale which you first heard played by an oboe in bar 112?

Anthology No. 34: Nationalism

1 In which key does this extract start and finish?

2 Upon which one of these scales is the piano introduction based: a), b), c), or d)?

    a) harmonic minor

    b) melodic minor

    c) major

    d) Dorian mode

3 Which string instrument has the main melodic line in bars 4-7?

4 Which instrument plays the bass part?

5 Follow the bass part as you listen to bars 5-9. Which one of these words best describes the harmonic progression in bars 5-9: a), b), c), or d)?

    a) discordant

    b) modal

    c) major

    d) atonal

6 In the same bars (5-9) which one of these words applies to the piano part: a), b), c), or d)?

    a) counter-melody

    b) fugue

    c) imitation

    d) answer

7 In bar 8 there is a false relation between the viola and the first violin. It produces a jarring effect rather like a 'blue' note. Which two notes cause this effect?

8 What does *sul G* mean in bar 23?

9 In which bars and on which instrument was the melody played by the first violin in bars 24-26 first heard?

10 In which bars does the final cadence of this extract occur? What sort of cadence is it?

Anthology No. 35: Orchestration, Melody and Tonality

LISTENING
WITHOUT
PRINTED
MUSIC

1 Name the first solo instrument.
2 Which of the following shapes corresponds to the notes of the beginning of this solo: a), b), c), or d)?

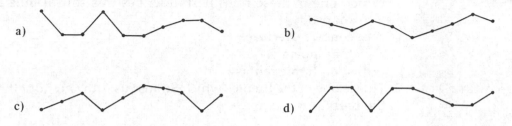

a)   b)

c)   d)

3 The first solo is joined by a clarinet in a duet. Which one of these terms correctly refers to the rich, dark sound of this instrument when it is played as it is in this duet, in its bottom octave: a), b), c), or d)?
   a) first position
   b) chalumeau register
   c) fundamental
   d) clarino register
4 Name the instrument which next plays a duet with the first solo instrument, over a throbbing string accompaniment.
5 At the end of the extract a short, partially unaccompanied phrase is heard on the clarinet. The same phrase is immediately repeated an octave lower. Which solo instrument plays this repeat?

LISTENING
WITH
PRINTED
MUSIC

1 The main key of this movement is D major, the key in which the first solo begins. What is unusual about the key of the first five bars?
2 In which bars do you hear the tonic pedal of an unrelated key?

[33]

Anthology No. 36: Programme Music

LISTENING
WITH
PRINTED
MUSIC

1 This extract is the final section of an orchestral piece in one movement. Strauss calls it an *Epilog*: what is the more usual term for such a concluding section?

2 The complete work describes the adventures of a mischievous folk hero. Which one of these titles best describes this sort of music: a), b), c), or d)?

    a) rhapsody

    b) concert overture

    c) tone poem

    d) symphonic fantasy

3 This is one of the themes which Strauss uses throughout the work to represent the hero:

In which bars of this *Epilog* can you hear this theme played

    a) as given above?

    b) slowly and quietly?

Which instrument plays just the first three notes of this theme four times?

4 Here is another of the themes representing the hero:

In which bars can you hear a version of this theme played three times? Which instruments play it?

5 Strauss is justly famed for his wonderful orchestration. Describe any single bar in which he uses the strings in an original and colourful manner.

Anthology No. 37: Harmony, Melody and Style

LISTENING
WITHOUT
PRINTED
MUSIC

1 On which scale are the harmonies and melodies based; is it: a), b), or c)?

    a) chromatic

    b) pentatonic

    c) whole-tone

2 What is the style of this music: a), b), or c)?

    a) Expressionist

    b) Impressionist

    c) Avant-garde

3 Describe the features of the music which led you to make your choice in question 2.

LISTENING
WITH
PRINTED
MUSIC

Listen all the way through the music several times before answering the following questions.

1 The melodies are all conjunct (moving by step) except in two bars. Which are these bars?

2 How are the melodies in the right and left hands in bars 10 and 11 related?

3 What type of chord is heard in the left-hand part of bar 15?

4 Three intervals are used more than any other in the harmonies and melodies. Which are they?

Anthology No. 38: Texture

LISTENING
WITHOUT
PRINTED
MUSIC

1 In which year do you think this piece might have been composed?

2 Which of these three terms best describes the texture: a), b), or c)?
   a) homophonic
   b) heterophonic
   c) polyphonic

3 The form of the example involves a clear shape as the player's hands go up and down the keyboard. Which of the following shapes most clearly resembles the music you can hear: a), b), or c)?

a)

b)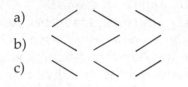

c)

LISTENING
WITH
PRINTED
MUSIC

1 After the opening chords there are two more points at which the chords cover the full compass of the piano. Identify those points using the numbered beats in the score.

2 Identify examples of a) ostinato,
                            b) a cluster chord,
                            c) a polyrhythm.

3 After the opening there is only one other bar-line (at 38). Suggest a reason why the composer put it there.

Anthology No. 39: Atonality

LISTENING
WITHOUT
PRINTED
MUSIC

1 This example consists of a theme and one of a set of variations. The teacher will play the theme several times. Although there are no melodies to guide you, you will hear that the theme is divided into short phrases, separated by rests. How many phrases are there?

LISTENING
WITH
PRINTED
MUSIC

1 The music in this example is based on a twelve-note row. It appears three times during the course of the theme (bars 1-12) in various forms. Listen to the theme again.
   a) In which bar and on which note does the first statement of the twelve-note row end?
   b) The next statement of the row begins immediately. In which bar and on which note does this one end?
   c) The notes of this statement are in a different order to the first one, but the two statements are closely related. Is the second one
      i) a retrograde version (i.e. played backwards), or
      ii) an inversion (with the intervals upside-down)?
   d) How is the second statement rhythmically related to the first?

2 Now listen to the music all the way through. In what ways does the composer introduce variation
   a) in the texture?
   b) in the rhythm?
   c) in the phrasing?

Anthology No. 40: Rhythm, Melody and Instrumentation

LISTENING WITHOUT PRINTED MUSIC

1 This piece involves the following percussion instruments: xylophone, side drum, bass drum, triangle, cymbal, gong and timpani. Which of them are heard in this example?
2 In how many sections is the example?
3 Of those sections, which do you think was the longest and which was the shortest?

LISTENING WITH PRINTED MUSIC

Listen to the opening melody several times. Then listen all the way through.

1 In which bars does the melody appear in canon?
2 How is it related to the melody which begins in bar 28?
3 How is it related to the melody which begins in bar 44?
4 The opening melody contains two rhythmic figures which are used as the basis of all the melodies. Write down the two rhythms.

Anthology No. 41: Atonality, Rhythm and Melody

LISTENING WITHOUT PRINTED MUSIC

1 Listen to the music all the way through. You will hear that the example is in two main sections. In what ways does the music of the second section differ from the first?
2 Listen again, concentrating on the violin melodies in the first section. Which of the three shapes below most clearly resembles the 'shape' of the melody: a), b), or c)?

a) ——————————

b) ⌣

c) ⌢

3 Now listen to Anthology No. 39. Both of these examples are atonal. In what ways do the approaches of the two composers differ?

LISTENING WITH PRINTED MUSIC

1 The opening melody in the violin part is rhythmically related to the pattern of harmonies which accompany it. In what way is it related?
2 Indicate three examples of melodic imitation in the second half of the example (beginning at bar 12).
3 At the start of this second half the instruments have the direction 'sul tasto'. What does this mean and what is its effect?
4 How, in the first section, has the composer indicated that the melody and the chords should be played differently?

Anthology No. 42: Melody and Form

LISTENING
WITHOUT
PRINTED
MUSIC

1 Which one of these terms most accurately describes the form of this movement: a), b), or c)?
   a) binary
   b) rondo
   c) ternary

2 The opening melody for two trumpets is repeated later in the movement. What has been added to the repeat?

LISTENING
WITH
PRINTED
MUSIC

1 Before listening, study the melody of the first bar carefully. The melody in the first bar is the basis of all the other melodies in the movement. Suggest some ways in which this melody is used and reused in the remainder of the opening theme?

2 In which bars does this melody appear
   a) in canon?
   b) in augmentation (with longer note values)?
   c) in inversion (upside down)?

3 Study bars 287^4-300. How has the composer treated the melody in this section?

4 Lastly, a question about the instruments. In bars 287 and 297 the double basses are pitched unusually high. How has the player achieved this effect?

Anthology No. 43: The Avant-garde, Form

LISTENING
WITHOUT
PRINTED
MUSIC

In this example the composer has transcribed a number of bird-songs. These alternate with groups of solemn chords.

1 How many different bird-songs do you think are represented?

2 How many chordal passages are there?

3 Listen carefully to the lengths of the bird-song and chordal passages. One gets shorter over the course of the example whilst the other gets longer. Do the chords get longer and the bird-songs shorter? Or the other way round?

LISTENING
WITH
PRINTED
MUSIC

1 Identify a) one example of a consonant bird-song,
       b) one example of a dissonant bird-song,
       c) two bird-songs whose intervals are related.

2 The composer has chosen not to include time signatures. Suggest a reason why these would not have been appropriate.

3 The chords feature one interval in particular. Which interval?

Anthology No. 44: Percussion Instruments, Indeterminacy and Notation

LISTENING
WITHOUT
PRINTED
MUSIC

1 There are nine different percussion instruments in this example. Name those that you can identify.
2 The instruments which are played most frequently all have something in common. What is it?

LISTENING
WITH
PRINTED
MUSIC

1 Listen carefully to the first fifteen 'bars' of the first page. In which order does the player perform the three short passages in the box above the stave?
2 Now listen all the way through. In the last box of all, the player does something unexpected with the short passages.
    a) In which order does he play them?
    b) What is unexpected about the playing of one of them?
3 Give an example of a) a graphic notation,
                        b) a proportional notation.
4 This piece can be played forwards or backwards. Turn your score upside down (which is what the player would have to do for a 'backwards' version). Some of the passages are the same no matter which way round they are played. Which are these passages?

Anthology No. 45: Graphic Scores

Listen to the first part of the example several times. Concentrate on the first three groups of sounds.

LISTENING
WITHOUT
PRINTED
MUSIC

1 Invent a notation for each of the following sounds.
    a) tick
    b) sigh
    c) dong

Now listen all the way through.
2 The various sounds, put together, depict a series of short scenes. In your own words, what do you think is happening in these scenes?

LISTENING
WITH
PRINTED
MUSIC

1 Compare your own notations for a tick, a sigh and a dong with the ones on the first page of the score. Why do you think the composer notated hers on a three-line stave?
2 On the third page of the score the graphics suggest the sound of a car starting up.
    a) Invent an alternative notation of your own for this sound.
    b) Try to notate the sound in *conventional* notation.
3 What changes would have to be made to the score if it were performed by a male singer?
4 Suggest some ways in which the closing scene could be acted out by one person on stage.

Anthology No. 46: Melody and Style

LISTENING
WITHOUT
PRINTED
MUSIC

1 At the opening you will hear a very Romantic-sounding melody played by the cello. This is then taken up by other instruments which transform it in a variety of ways. How many transformations are there?
2 In the second half of the example there is an 'instrument' not commonly heard in a music ensemble. What is it?
3 The opening cello melody is repeated towards the end. What is unusual about the repeat?

LISTENING
WITH
PRINTED
MUSIC

1 In which bars does the composer quote from an earlier style of music? Could you suggest a date for this style?
2 Listen carefully to the flute and basset clarinet melody starting in bar 263. This melody is related to the opening melody, and the melodies in the section beginning at bar 280. Suggest some ways in which these melodies might be related.
3 The teacher will explain the legend of St Veronica. How do you think the composer has referred to this legend in musical terms?

Anthology No. 47: Electronic Music and Rhythm

LISTENING
WITHOUT
PRINTED
MUSIC

Note This is a piece of electronic music for which there is no score.

1 This piece is all about time. What common sounds does the composer treat electronically to represent this?
2 How many sections are there in the example?
3 Which of these sections do you think is the longest?
   Make a list of the sections and write down your estimated timings.
   Now listen again with a stop-watch and note the exact timings.
   Are these different from your first impression?
   Suggest some reasons why there may have been differences.
4 The opening consists of a slow ostinato.
   a) Try to write down the rhythm.
   b) What happens to the rhythm of this ostinato after a few 'bars'?
5 In what respects is the last group of sounds different from the first: is it
   a) higher or lower?
   b) faster or slower?
   c) the same or different in timbre (tone quality)?
6 Now that you have probably guessed what the 'common sounds' referred to in question 1 are, compare the electronic effects used on each of them.
   a) Describe the effect of the electronic treatment of the first sounds.
   b) Describe the effect of the electronic treatment of the last sounds.

Anthology No. 48: Texture

LISTENING WITHOUT PRINTED MUSIC

1 This piece involves an instrument not commonly heard in the concert hall, and not associated with electronic music. What is the instrument?

2 The music of the example is all based on a simple melody which can be heard quite clearly at various points.

    a) What style of melody is it?

    b) Suggest a time signature for the melody.

    c) In what respects does its rhythm differ from the other melodic figures in the example?

3 Describe in your own words what happens to the melody at the end.

4 Describe in your own words the type of counterpoint which results from the combination of instrument and tape.

LISTENING WITH PRINTED MUSIC

1 In which bars can you hear a drone?

2 Are the drones played by the instrument or are they on tape?

3 In which bar can you clearly hear the melody referred to in question 2 of the 'Listening without printed music' section being played on tape?

4 Explain in your own words what is happening to the rhythm of this melody in bar 81.

Anthology No. 49: Instrumentation, Style and Form

LISTENING WITHOUT PRINTED MUSIC

1 This song is taken from a piece of music which was originally composed for the concert hall. Why is it unusual that a song in this style should have been included in a concert?

2 The song is in five sections: Introduction, Bridge, Chorus, Verse 1, Verse 2. Describe, in your own words, the difference between a bridge, a chorus and a verse.

3 The opening chord sounds as if it is being played by a full orchestra. In fact, it is played by a solo instrument. What type of modern instrument can copy the sounds of others? (Clue: a synthesizer can, but there is another which is even more accurate.)

LISTENING WITH PRINTED MUSIC

1 Suggest a name to describe the type of synthesizer sound used to play each of the following passages.

    a) the melody beginning in bar 9

    b) the melody beginning in bar 17

    c) the bass part

2 Some of the instrumental parts heard in this example have been sequenced.

    a) What is a sequencer?

    b) Identify two parts which sound as if they have been sequenced.

    c) In what ways does a sequenced part differ from the performance given by a 'live' musician?

3 Your teacher will explain the term MIDI.

Suggest some ways in which the technique of MIDI would have helped the composer of this example to put the song together.

Anthology No. 50: Melody and Instrumental Techniques

LISTENING WITHOUT PRINTED MUSIC

1 In the guitar introduction the notes of the melody are joined by glissandi. How do you think this effect is produced?
2 Listen to the music all the way through, concentrating on the verses which follow the spoken introduction.
   a) How many verses are there?
   b) How many bars are there in each verse?
3 What term would you use to describe the guitar accompaniment?
4 Here is the 'blues' scale upon which the melody is based:

   a) Mark the degrees of the scale which are sung as 'blue' notes.
   b) The guitar introduction includes a 'blue' note which is chromatic and not part of this scale. Next to which degree of the scale does it appear?

LISTENING WITH PRINTED MUSIC

1 The rhythm of the guitar introduction is different from that of the vocal melody. In what way is the rhythm different?
2 The verse includes at least one bar in which a new harmony is suggested, but which is not played in the accompaniment. Identify the bar.

Anthology No. 51: Rhythm and Harmony

LISTENING WITHOUT PRINTED MUSIC

1 The example consists of an eight-bar introduction followed by a series of improvisations. Listen several times until you are sure you know when the first verse begins.
   The three wind players (clarinet, trumpet and trombone) take it in turn to lead the improvisation. Write down the order in which you can hear them.

LISTENING WITH PRINTED MUSIC

1 Identify examples of: a) a 'lean' (when a phrase begins a beat late)
                        b) a 'push' (when a note is played just before you expect it).
2 Which bars of the verse (which starts in bar 9) constitute the turnaround?
3 Listen carefully, with the score, to the clarinet in the first four bars of the verse (bars 9-12). Write down the main melody notes so as to indicate what the 'straight' version of the melody might be.
4 Listen to the music all the way through several times.
   a) At which bar does the trombone start a completely new melody?
   b) Which bars does the clarinet player vary most often over the course of the verses?

Anthology No. 52: Instrumentation, Style and Harmony

LISTENING
WITHOUT
PRINTED
MUSIC

1 What are the names of the three instruments which play the solos?
2 Which of the following terms most accurately describes the style of the music: a), b), or c)?
   a) blues
   b) ragtime
   c) jazz
3 Each of the solos has its own character. Which one
   a) employs many jazz quavers and semiquavers?
   b) sounds as if it is being played by a classically trained musician?
   c) is made up of short, two-bar phrases?

LISTENING
WITH
PRINTED
MUSIC

1 What is the harmony of the introduction?
2 Identify three bars in which there is a 'stop'.
3 Identify two bars in which there is a 'blue' note.
4 The chords of the piano part in bars 3-6 are written out below. Which notes have been added to the root, third and fifth in order to create a more jazzy effect?

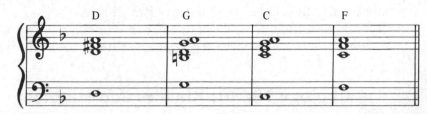

Anthology No. 53: Harmony and Texture

LISTENING
WITHOUT
PRINTED
MUSIC

1 Listen carefully to the bass line of bars 1-9. It is based on a simple arpeggio pattern.
   a) On which beat of the bar is the *root* of the chord played?
   b) On which beat of the bar is the *third* played?
2 Which instrument is playing repeated chords?
3 The backing vocalists use two vowel sounds. One is 'ooh'. What sound does it change to later in the verse?

LISTENING
WITH
PRINTED
MUSIC

1 Which note of the harmony (not necessarily consonant) is the lead vocalist singing on the first beat of each of the following bars?
   a) bar 8
   b) bar 11
   c) bar 17
2 Suggest a chord symbol to describe the dissonant jazz chord in the final bar. You will need to work out which notes belong to a chord of F major and which do not.

[42]

Anthology No. 54: Harmony and Melody

LISTENING WITHOUT PRINTED MUSIC

1 Extra interest has been added to the arrangement by changing the key at various points.
   a) At what point in the verses does this happen?
   b) How many times does it happen?
2 Listen carefully to the bass part.
   a) Why do you think this type of bass part is called a 'walking bass'?
   b) Suggest some different types of melodic figuration which a player might use to create such an effect.

LISTENING WITH PRINTED MUSIC

1 List some of the features which identify this example as 'swing' jazz.
2 Listen carefully with the score to the vocal melody. Because it is a jazz version of a much simpler melody its rhythms are more complicated. Write down on the stave below what you think the first four bars of the original might have sounded like.

3 Listen to the example, concentrating on the piano part. Identify at least two bars in which the pianist adds a passing jazz harmony.

Anthology No. 55: Rhythm and Melody

LISTENING WITHOUT PRINTED MUSIC

Before you listen to the example clap the following rhythms, which are taken from it, so as to familiarize yourself with them:

1 In which instrumental parts do these rhythms appear?
   a)...
   b) ....
   c)...

LISTENING WITH PRINTED MUSIC

Listen carefully to the melody all the way through. You will notice that there is one verse of vocal melody followed by two played by the saxophone, then a new section.

1 Which bars of the saxophone melody most closely resemble the original vocal line?
2 Which bars of the saxophone melody are the least like the original?
3 In the new section, beginning at bar 25, there is a melodic sequence.
   a) How many sequential phrases are there?
   b) In which bars do they begin?

Anthology No. 56: Rhythmic Figuration and Harmony

LISTENING
WITHOUT
PRINTED
MUSIC

1 Listen to the brass parts. They play a short phrase which is repeated through-out the song. What is the pop term for such a figure?

2 After two verses there is a middle section during which a part of this figure moves to a different beat of the bar.

The rhythm of the figure is: ♫♩

To which beat does it move?

3 For most of the song the guitar plays the chords on two particular beats of the bar. Which beats are they?

4 Each of the verses is in twelve-bar blues form. Listen to the first verse several times, then answer the following questions:
   a) The first chord is F (in roman numerals, I). What are the other two chords which make up this twelve-bar sequence?
   b) In which order do these chords appear?
   c) What is the harmony of the 'stop' bar, in which the singer sings unac-companied?

Anthology No. 57: Style, Harmony and Rhythm

LISTENING
WITHOUT
PRINTED
MUSIC

1 What effect is the guitarist using which is typical of 'heavy' rock?

2 What is the interval being played by the guitar and bass at the beginning? (Clue: it is an unusual one in rock music.)

3 The drum pattern heard at the beginning is written out below with the bass drum part missing. Fill in the rhythm.

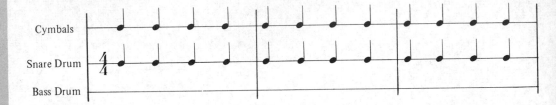

4 The verse consists of three chords, spread over two bars and repeated. The chords are F minor, A flat and B flat.
   a) How many beats does the F minor chord occupy?
   b) On which beat of the bar does the third chord appear?

LISTENING
WITH
PRINTED
MUSIC

1 Identify two bars in which there are examples of
   a) a 'push',
   b) a fill,
   c) a riff,
   d) a cymbal punctuating the phrase.

2 Write out the note names of the 'blue' scale on which the melodies and harmonies are based.

Anthology No. 58: Melody and Arrangement

LISTENING
WITHOUT
PRINTED
MUSIC

1 This is a rock arrangement for a large orchestra, although it includes at least two instruments normally found in a rock band. Name the instruments.

2 The arrangement builds up over two vocal verses. Write a brief summary of the instruments and voices used.

LISTENING
WITH
PRINTED
MUSIC

1 Listen to the example, concentrating on the first bar of the vocal melody (bar 10). Now listen again, concentrating this time on the melodies played by the orchestra and choir. Using bar numbers identify examples of each of the following:

    a) an inversion of the phrase (i.e. a descending phrase) in the trumpet part

    b) two augmentations (i.e. with longer note values) in the violin parts –
       (Clue: one is more augmented than the other)

    c) an augmented version in the choir parts

2 Identify two examples of a pedal bass.

Anthology No. 59: Harmony, Instrumental and Recording Techniques

LISTENING
WITHOUT
PRINTED
MUSIC

1 In which instrumental parts are there examples of:

    a) echo?

    b) comping?

    c) a fill?

2 A drum machine is employed for a particular sound on the recording. What is the sound and on which beats of the bar does it appear?

LISTENING
WITH
PRINTED
MUSIC

1 The piano solo at the start is based upon a four-bar chord sequence (bars 1-4, repeated in bars 5-8). With which type of cadence does this sequence end: is it

    a) imperfect?

    b) perfect?

    c) interrupted?

2 Listen to the vocal chorus.

    a) How many chords make up this chorus section?

    b) Upon which words of the lyric do the chord changes occur?

3 With which type of cadence does the chord sequence of the chorus end: is it

    a) imperfect?

    b) perfect?

    c) interrupted?

Anthology No. 60: Style and Recording Techniques

LISTENING WITHOUT PRINTED MUSIC

1 There are many features which identify this example as reggae. What, in particular, is characteristic of
   a) the harmony?
   b) the words?
   c) the rhythm of the guitar part?
   d) the rhythm of the bass part?
   e) the drumming technique?

2 In which instrumental parts are each of the following recording techniques used?
   a) echo
   b) overlay
   c) reverberation

3 The following are heard on the recording: vocals, violin, guitar, bass guitar, percussion and drums. Listen carefully to the recording mix. Some parts are more prominent than others. Place them in order of prominence.

LISTENING WITH PRINTED MUSIC

1 At bar 9 there is a 'dub' section.
   a) Explain what is meant by the term 'dub'.
   b) To which instruments on this recording has the technique been applied?

Anthology No. 61: Rhythm, Melody and Instrumental Effects

LISTENING WITHOUT PRINTED MUSIC

1 Listen carefully to the drum part building up in the introduction. The back-beat is added after the fourth bar. On which drum is it played and on which beats of the bar?

2 In which parts are the following effects employed:
   a) wah-wah?
   b) reverberation?

LISTENING WITH PRINTED MUSIC

1 Listen carefully to the bass riff which is repeated at the beginning.
   How are the notes of this riff related to:
   a) the short guitar solo in bar 7?
   b) the vocal melody starting in bar 9?
   c) the bass and guitar parts in bar 9?

2 The introduction (up to bar 9) features a particular style of bass playing. What is the term given to this style?

3 The bass guitarist uses three different ways of playing the instrument over the course of bars 7-9. What are they?

4 Now listen to the vocal verses. The bass and guitar parts play a rhythmic phrase which then repeats throughout the rest of the song. How many bars long is this phrase?

Anthology No. 62

LISTENING
WITHOUT
PRINTED
MUSIC

1 Which two Indonesian countries feature this type of orchestra?
2 Which instruments make up the orchestra?
3 Which of the following Western terms most closely describes the texture of the music: a), b), or c)?
   a) polyphonic
   b) homophonic
   c) heterophonic
4 Describe some of the ways in which the form of the music is different from Western forms that you know.

Anthology No. 63

LISTENING
WITHOUT
PRINTED
MUSIC

1 At the beginning of the recorded example you can hear the leader of the drummers calling instructions to the rest of the players. In what ways do you think his role might be different to that of a Western orchestral conductor?
2 The drums are played in many different ways. List some of the different ways that you can hear in the example.
3 In what ways are the rhythms different from European popular music?
4 Western musicians find it very difficult to write down the rhythms of African drums. Suggest some reasons why this might be.
5 Try to guess how many different drummers are playing in this example.

Anthology No. 64

LISTENING
WITHOUT
PRINTED
MUSIC

1 This music is Japanese. Which of the following styles of music do you think it is: a), b), or c)?
   a) folk
   b) popular
   c) classical
2 At the very beginning you will hear a group of instruments. Do you think these instruments are:
   a) playing an overture?
   b) playing the main melody?
   c) tuning up?
3 After the opening you will hear a melody played by the flute. In between the phrases you will hear percussion instruments.
   a) How many different flute phrases are played?
   b) How many different percussion instruments can you hear?
   c) In what ways is the use of percussion different from anything you have heard in Western music?
4 After the flute solo a new instrument plays a melody. Which of the following types of instrument is it: a), b), or c)?
   a) string
   b) brass
   c) woodwind

Anthology No. 65

LISTENING
WITHOUT
PRINTED
MUSIC

1 Which country do you think this example is from?
2 What type of string instrument is playing in the example?
3 How do you think the player produces the 'twanging' effect?
4 How many drums are playing in the example?
5 There are two contrasting sections. What is different about
    a) the instrumentation?
    b) the rhythm?
    c) the melody?
6 The music of this country uses a particular type of melody. What is the name given to the melody?

Anthology No. 66

LISTENING
WITHOUT
PRINTED
MUSIC

1 What is the name of the instrument which is playing the drone?
2 Of what material is this instrument made?
3 Describe how you think the player produces the sound.
4 Which types of instruments, apart from the drone, can you hear on the recording?
5 This example is a piece of dance music. There are several features which are similar to dance music in many other parts of the world. What are these features?

Anthology No. 67

LISTENING
WITHOUT
PRINTED
MUSIC

1 This is an example of Chinese chamber music. What is chamber music and what features do you think this example has in common with Western chamber music?
2 On what type of scale is the music based: is it
    a) chromatic?
    b) modal?
    c) whole-tone?
    d) pentatonic?
3 How many different instruments are playing?
4 What type of instruments are they?
5 Describe how the melody is divided between the instruments.
6 An important feature of Chinese music is the way in which an ascending phrase is balanced by a descending one. Listen carefully to the whole of the example then listen again with a pencil and paper. Try to count the number of each type of phrase. Are there an equal number?

Anthology No. 68

1 The following list of instruments includes one which is *not* heard in this example. Which one is it: a), b), c), d) or e)?
   a) bowed string
   b) plucked string
   c) reed
   d) flute
   e) drum
2 The main melody instrument is a dulcimer. What is a dulcimer and how is it played?
3 How many different melodic phrases are there in the example?
4 The form of this example, which is from Iran, is based on classical Persian poetry. One of the features of the poems is that the lines are written in pairs. In what ways is this suggested in the music?
5 Name two features of this music which are very like Western music and two features which are very unlike it.

Anthology No. 69

1 What are the two instruments playing the melody?
2 What is the principal instrument playing the chords?
3 What are the features of the melody and rhythm which would lead you to think that the musicians were improvising?
4 There is no conductor, yet the accompanying musicians all seem to know when to change the harmony. Suggest some ways in which the soloist might be giving them 'clues'. Are these 'clues': a), b), or c)?
   a) in the melody
   b) in the rhythm
   c) in both

1 The instrument on the second line is a *taragot*. To which common Western orchestral instrument is it related?
2 Listen carefully to the trills being played on the two solo instruments. Some of them are very unlike the trills heard in Western Classical music, but what is different about them?
3 Listen carefully to the harmonies on the first page of the score. What is unusual about one of them?

Anthology No. 70

1 From which continent does this example come?
2 What type of instrument is playing the melody and how many different types are there in the example?
3 Suggest some ways in which this music might have been influenced by Spanish music.

1 In which bars is the melody lengthened by two extra beats?
2 The chords on the last beat of bars 14-16 are substitute chords. Name the common harmony they replace.
3 What is the key relationship between the first sixteen bars and the last sixteen bars?

Anthology No. 71

1 What type of instruments are playing this music and from which island do they come?
2 The names of the instruments are given below. Place them in order, starting with the highest in pitch.
    a) guitar
    b) boom
    c) ping-pong
    d) cello

Listen to the example several times before answering the following questions.
1 Using bar numbers, identify two places which suggest the style of European classical music.
2 Now identify one place which suggests jazz and one which suggests disco.
3 In bars 9 and 10 the melody notes in the second line are being played in a special way. What technique is the player using?
4 Identify two bars in which there are unexpected changes of harmony.